Restoring Broken Walls

A Prison Ministry Exposition of Isaiah 61

Philip Ireson

Senior Chaplain, HMP and YOI Doncaster

GROVE BOOKS LIMITED
RIDLEY HALL RD CAMBRIDGE CB3 9HU

Contents

The Cover Illustration is by Peter Ashton

Copyright © Philip Ireson 2004

First Impression January 2004
ISSN 1470-8531
ISBN 1 85174 553 X

Introduction

1

At the regular early morning prayer meeting in the Chapel of St Barnabas in HMP Doncaster an elderly prisoner stood up with trembling hands as he read out a personal testimony.

He had not been to church for many years. He had never expected to come to prison and he was desperately worried that his family had disowned him. Another prisoner had invited him to chapel. God had touched the man's life in a powerful and beautiful way and he had given his life to Christ.

> The newspapers report mostly on controversies within the church... but something else is taking place at the grassroots level—below the grassroots level, even, in societies' 'garbage-heaps.' In Northern Ireland, former IRA terrorists now take communion alongside Protestants they once had sworn to kill. In Papua New Guinea, prison ministry is led by a judge who used to sentence people to the jails he now visits in the name of Christ.[1]

Bishop Desmond Tutu has said that the Western world would experience a 'spiritual bankruptcy' if it were deprived of the 'moral capital' of its prisoners. Tutu traces a lineage which includes John Bunyan, Gandhi, Luther King and Solzhenitsyn. A by-product of prison ministries is the remarkable opportunity to minister to the future leaders of the world.

During the last ten years the prison population in the UK has increased from 50,000 to 74,000 people. During the same decade church attendance declined steadily, so much so that newspapers began to predict the imminent demise of the institution. Alongside the decline

A by-product of prison ministries is the remarkable opportunity to minister to the future leaders of the world

of most Christian denominations in the 1990s, it seems to me that there has been an overwhelming move towards introspection and an over-analysis of church structures and organization. As someone ordained nearly 20 years ago I wonder what has happened to the prophets in the church.

I do not find it a comfortable time to be in the Church of England. I am not paid by the organization any more as I work for a private company which manages prisons but I am proud to belong, to keep my ordination vows and to be under the authority of a local church. However, I cannot help thinking that the wider church has lost sight of God and his sweeping purposes for the 'poor' and the exiled, the sick and the lame.

During a year at HMP Doncaster we briefly see 5,000 men—mostly under the age of 25, and mostly from a low income group—and we probably get to know about a hundred of them in depth as they join our chapel community during the year before moving on. It is salutary to note that with the exception of four men, in the past two years not one of these 5,000 men reports having had previous contact with the Church of England and its vaunted parish system. Many of them recognize a 'vicar' but that is probably more to do with the Vicar of Dibley than anything the Church of England has managed to pass onto them. Yet many believe in God and want prayer and a better future, a hundred come to chapel each Sunday, many listening seriously and thirstily, and many of them are ready to take the radical step of believing. This situation is repeated in many of the prisons of this country and across the world.

Many of them recognize a 'vicar' but that is probably more to do with the Vicar of Dibley than the C of E

So, it is with both sadness and hope that I write this booklet, looking again at what the Bible, rather than the church, has to offer. It is a journey that begins with Isaiah 61, a prophecy given to a nation which was disappointed—disappointed with itself and with its institutions, scared of the future but with a lingering hope that a faithful God still cared for his people and would act. It is hardly surprising that the Scriptures given to these people have been a rich vein to be mined in search of the hidden riches promised for those who seek, so that 'You may know that it is I, the Lord, the God of Israel, who call you by name' (Isaiah 45.3).

So why choose the prophet Isaiah rather than a New Testament theme of renewal and the Holy Spirit? Listening to George Lings of Church Army talking on the future of the church in the 21st century I was struck by his thesis that Old Testament passages such as Isaiah 61 are the ones which God is pressing onto his church at this time.[2] It seems no coincidence that it was Isaiah

So why choose the prophet Isaiah rather than a New Testament theme of renewal and the Holy Spirit?

61 from which Jesus quoted (Luke 4) as he began his mission to a weary people tired of defeat and retreat and whose leaders taught without authority.

Indeed, I am not the first person to follow this journey—the writings of the exiled and post-exilic people of God have been a source of inspiration to many during times of watching, waiting and wondering and for those suffering and being persecuted. As Simeon watched and waited for the Messiah he would probably have turned to passages such as Isaiah 53 and 61, known to him by heart.

In my journey through Isaiah I take the generally held position that in chapter 61 we are dealing with post-exilic writings which link with the Jewish history of Ezra-Nehemiah and the prophecies from writers such as Haggai. I also assume that the people of God through faith in Christ are inheritors of all the promises and warnings which we find in Isaiah and other prophetic writings in the Old Testament. Quotations used come from the Revised Standard Version.

This is a journey which we have taken together in St Barnabas chapel at HMP Doncaster over the last few months. In this booklet I will sketch out the understanding that has been developed together. I have illustrated this with real life stories. Initials are used but I have been careful not to be sensationalist; prison testimonies are tricky things and circumstances change. At the time of writing each person described is 'walking the talk'—which means doing what they say. Please remember that I am writing as a representative of the prison community and so I ask you not to be surprised at the straightforward nature of this text. Christian ministry in prison is both immediate and direct.

This is a journey which we have taken together in St Barnabas chapel at HMP Doncaster

2

'The Spirit of the Lord has anointed me to preach good news to the poor.'

I like the straightforwardness of this statement. Jesus took these words as his manifesto at the beginning of his ministry and I believe that the same words apply to us as we humbly follow in his footsteps. The statement does not say, '*May* anoint me' nor does it qualify itself with a sub-clause with reference to appendix F! Time and time again early Christian teachers such as Paul make it quite clear in their teachings on the Holy Spirit that the Spirit *in action not theory* is the possession of every Christian (for example Ephesians 1.13–14).

In the Chapel of St Barnabas at Doncaster prison we set out aiming to see the Holy Spirit in action. We realize that we are sinful human beings in need of God's grace. We accept that we will make a mess of things and get confused but we also accept the glorious and grace-full action of a God who anoints us with his Spirit. How the church needs to rediscover that joyful freedom!

My writing has just been interrupted by a phone call from one of our volunteer chaplains, Steve. Steve is a businessman who freely gives up his time each Monday afternoon to lead a Bible study group and then visit one or two prisoners. He has just rung to tell me about two conversations he has just had on the Health Care wing of the prison. One of them, which lasted for an hour, was with one of our chapel men, J. I bumped into J a few months ago on a corridor shortly after he had arrived in the prison. J had been charged with some very serious offences and he told me that he had been desperate to be caught and that he needed to come to chapel. A little later on he duly appeared. This was the first peace he had had for years, he told us. Slowly J thawed out, rediscovered the gift of music and drank thirstily from the water of life.

A few weeks ago he started to exhibit terrible anger towards himself which resulted in a desperate attempt at suicide one afternoon on the wing after returning from a Bible group. He was taken to Health Care and placed on a suicide watch. As Steve talked with him about his impulsive and destructive behaviour J asked why this was happening to him. Why the swing between blessedness and despair? After the conversation J's cell mate also asked for a chat. A sad story of childhood abuse emerged, his father had injected him with heroin at the age of eleven, and a fatal road crash and hopelessness at least was wrapped round some positive knowledge imparted at a little Sunday school some years before. Steve shared the Good News with the young man and prayed with him, promising to return. Remember that if J had not been in the cell with A the conversation would never have happened. Despite his difficulties, J now has the opportunity to put into practice the fact that he is anointed with the Spirit to proclaim more of the Good News to A.

Anointing takes place in response to those God-given opportunities that abound every day.

We expect this kind of thing to happen every day. It feels like a Jesus ministry. We expect that a new convert *will be* anointed by the Spirit. I remember reading once that a person who had been a convert for six months in Singapore was considered to be a mature Christian. It seemed a bit shocking and dangerous but now I can see what that means. A re-reading of Acts brought home the results of the anointing of the Spirit on Paul. He often sped around, sometimes taught for as little as three days, appointed elders and was usually thrown out of the city shortly after. At best he might return for a few days or at least write a letter. He was convinced that what the Lord had begun he would continue and finish, the ultimate Mastermind. The message to the church *is to trust in the anointing*. Train by all means but trust in the anointing for out of that flows everything else. Trust and act. Why make the action of the Spirit so complicated? I marvel at the weighty tomes I see on the spiritual life with their diagrams and 39 steps and also the latest edict that to be a clergyman in the Anglican church you need a degree.

Questions for Reflection

1   Have there been occasions recently when you have experienced the anointing of the Spirit to help you perform a task?

2   Are there any occasions when you chose to ignore the prompting of the Spirit?

3   Are there any areas in which you would like to see the anointing of the Spirit?

3   Anointed to Bring Good Tidings

I met D about a year ago after he had been released from a long prison sentence on a two year licence.

He showed me his life story, written in beautiful English, even though D had not learned to write until he was an adult. He carried the terrible physical and mental scars from a lifetime of institutions and of abuse. D had suffered a quite horrific life. He had been taught as a child that it was wrong to laugh. His prison history was punctuated with long periods in segregation. His tattooed arms became so scarred by the long slashes he cut in them that he had needed plastic surgery. His life in prison echoed strongly Legion, the man who was chained in a graveyard and cut himself.

Three years ago he became a Christian in Preston after taking part in a Christian life skills course. Quite soon afterwards his new-found faith was tested to the core when he went out to see his dying mother. Attached to a long chain he was left alone with her but the pain of watching the skeleton-like body of his mother lying drugged in bed was too much for him to bear. Accompanied by two prison officers to her funeral, D shouted out at the clergyman taking the service and nearly sparked a major incident.

Last Christmas D was recalled on licence and came in to HMP Doncaster. Subsequently he told me that he was thinking of suicide—such was the crushing weight of his past, his sense of failure and his hopelessness. Then the chaplain appeared at the door. D decided to give life another go and the roller coaster began! D appeared in chapel shy, withdrawn and fearful of anyone who spoke to him, but gradually he came out of his shell and with encouragement began to take part in the early morning prayer and praise meetings which are a feature of life in St Barnabas Chapel. He eventually took the Thursday morning communion service: a broken member of the community, healed by the love of God, now recognized as one of the leaders of the community, holding up the broken bread as a sign of the sacrifice of Jesus, also broken, also suffering and also raised from the dead.

Then with great hope D was released into community, on licence after a long time in prison. Within three weeks he was returned to prison, having fallen, and full of remorse, self-condemnation and a deep sense of failure. But the pattern of forgiveness, of a future hope and an accepting God were now so ingrained in his heart and soul that quickly he sought forgiveness and absolution and wiser now has settled down to growing in his faith and preparing better when he is released again in ten months' time. Now, he laughs, plays practical jokes and his smile is a testimony to the year of the Lord's favour.

The release of the captives takes time and is a road marked with potholes and the occasional cul-de-sac and wrong turning—just like the people of Israel, sinful, wayward, but capable of great acts of faith. I am sure that the Father thinks of these broken ones in the same way.

Questions for Reflection

1   What kind of Christian environment does a prisoner like D require on release?

2   What kind of pitfalls could he experience?

3   How would your church be able to help him?

Anointed to Proclaim   4

'Anointed to proclaim the year of our Lord's favour and the day of vengeance of our God.'

Verse 8 amplifies this, 'For I the Lord love justice, I hate robbery and wrong.' Current political thought continually veers towards longer sentences and punishment. How can a Chaplaincy steer the middle road between forgiveness and healing and a rightful payment for wrong committed? We do this by proclaiming that God is totally opposed to wrongdoing. We emphasize the need for a truthful admission of wrong and an honest and courageous facing of the consequences. Maybe community revival follows on from repentance and an awesome awareness of the cost of sin.

C began to come to our groups. We were wary of him. His face was vicious and we discovered stories of robbery, violence and hate. He told us with a cold matter-of-factness in his voice that if a shop-owner did not respond immediately to his requests he would jump over the counter and immediately commit a violent act. But he kept on coming to chapel and we could not keep him away. One day he came to me complaining that at a recent court appearance the jury had only taken half an hour to convict him. 'Did you do the crimes?' I asked him. I could see that the very act of telling the truth was a deeply disturbing one for him. Eventually he said, 'Yes.'

Over the weeks with us C began to admit to some of the bad things he had done. Just before he left us to go to another prison he stood in front of an *Alpha* group and said, 'I admit that many of the things I have done have traumatized people, I sleep quietly in my bed in a way which they may never be able to.' Another, S, decided after one *Alpha* session to change his plea to guilty. And another ex-offender M, converted in Wolds prison, decided while in prison to clear the slate completely. He called the police for an interview and declining a solicitor told them everything.

Jesus said, 'The truth will set you free.' So Isaiah 61 gives us a template; God bestows favour but he also requires justice. As we are anointed by his Spirit, part of our task is to proclaim this message. All great movements of God have been accompanied by a fall in the crime rate![3]

Questions for Reflection

1   What is your attitude to God's judgment and justice?

2   Do you share the view that longer sentences reduce crime?

Anointed to Comfort 5

'To comfort all who mourn, to grant to those who mourn in Zion—to give them a garland instead of mourning.'

This is a task which the church still does well. No one else wants to talk about death, dying and grief but across the land Christians take this task upon themselves. The church needs to realize that it is the Spirit who anoints for this task and therefore we should expect to see him powerfully at work amongst the bereaved.

This is a task which the church still does well

For the past two years we have run a bereavement group at the prison. Every Thursday morning Marise, a volunteer from a local church, comes in and puts the kettle on. We send out invitations to a number of prisoners who are referred to us with bereavement issues. We never quite know who to expect. The group is not specifically Christian but inevitably God slips in and we are not self-conscious about mentioning his name. The anointing of the Spirit means that there is a total naturalness about this. In the group we look at the bereavement process and help the men to begin to understand why they are still caught in despair years after the death of a loved one. We find time and time again that no one has helped them do this. Maybe in years gone by the communities at work and at home would have provided the means to cry, to mourn safely and to journey through grief, but a computer screen or TV will not do this. Where do people meet now? A dominant thrust of much contemporary culture is to be self-sufficient, to be strong and not to admit to weakness; this is having a catastrophic effect on the inner lives of men. So we help them to talk about their self-harm and suicide attempts. It seems entirely right to provide a safe place in chapel where these ultimate questions and deep emotions can be safely expressed and explored.

A dominant thrust of much contemporary culture is to be self-sufficient and not to admit to weakness

Marise, whose husband died eight years ago in the most tragic way, is able to 'get alongside' the men—just as the Holy Spirit comes alongside us. 'The one who gets alongside us,' the *paracletos*, is the one who anoints us *to come alongside others.* There is a beautiful symmetry at work in us who believe. Marise has found a growing confidence in her work outside the prison as a church warden, 50 men have begun to experience healing, some have found faith—none more so than D who now offers the comfort with which he was comforted (2 Cor 1.4). A beautiful symmetry indeed.

Questions for Reflection

1 Reflect on the bereavement work you do.

2 Have there been times when your work has seemed to be particularly anointed by the Holy Spirit?

3 Are there ways in which contacts made through this kind of work could be encouraged to a deeper awareness of God?

6

Anointed to be
Oaks of Righteousness

Have you thought why God wants people to become Christians?

No doubt to be saved from hell, to be put right with God and to be given the gift of eternal life but Isaiah 61 adds another reason to this towering list: *'That they may become oaks of righteousness, the planting of the Lord.'*

It is a wonderful picture; God anoints you with the Spirit to proclaim the Good News but then those who respond become oaks of righteousness. The acorn of faith is planted in a soul, it is watered by prayer, nurtured by faith and then sprouts into a young seedling. Oak seedlings grow fast in the right conditions and within ten years an oak tree can be ten feet tall. At St Barnabas we see rapid growth when a man becomes a Christian. One year in chapel is perhaps equivalent to three in a church outside the walls. It is a veritable spiritual hothouse.

R came to chapel on 10th April 2002. He came along to have a look. A talented musician, he had lapsed into a drug habit which had destroyed his relationships, estranging him from his son and his parents. We needed an organist in chapel so he offered to play for us. His technical ability was such that he was able to sight read and quickly he was drawn to some of the modern songs we regularly sing, such as 'Faithful one,' 'When I look into your holiness.' Before long he had given his life to Christ and then the acorn sprouted and began to grow rapidly. It was a lovely thing to see him discover the great hymns which he had never heard before, including 'The day thou gavest Lord,' 'I cannot tell,' 'Blessed assurance.'

After a few months R stood up at one morning service and hesitantly gave his testimony in front of the gathered crowd. 'The biggest difference in my life now is that I have a conscience,' he told us. Since that point R has continued to grow in the gifts of the Spirit. Last Christmas he was anointed by the Spirit to tell another friend about his faith. G duly came on an *Alpha* course and became a Christian. R is now enjoying release at Beacon House, a Christian halfway home. He has begun to play music at local churches. His sense of humour and infectious enthusiasm are still there and are just some of the leaves growing fruitfully on this particular oak of righteousness.

We are reminded that trees which are planted in the word of God will never dry up and will provide fruit for the healing of the nations (Revelation 22.2). These trees, these redeemed lives, are a planting of the Lord that he may be glorified. This reinforces Desmond Tutu's words at the beginning of this booklet about the moral capital of the nation—and the church—being built up in the prisons. The Good News of the Lord's favour is to clothe the mournful poor with the mantle of praise instead of a faint spirit. At a recent service at my local church we prayed for residents and staff of Beacon House. As we gathered around them, a memorable picture was given to an elderly member of the congregation. She saw trees growing out from the church, strong and straight. We saw this as confirmation from the Lord that his purpose is to anoint broken and faint hearts, so that they can truly be oaks of righteousness, the planting of the Lord.

Questions for Reflection

1 If an ex-offender came to your church how would you help him or her to grow in faith?
2 Is there anything about your fellowship which might hinder this growth?

7 Anointed to Restore Broken Walls

In almost every other interview that we conduct lurks the tale of a sad and shameful episode of sexual or physical abuse.

I heard one young man's story that made me weep with shame because a representative of the church had been the abuser. As a vulnerable 13-year-old in the care of a religious-based care home he had suffered two years of domination by the principal who singled him out for special attention and favours. The young man had never told his story to anyone before. A dominant emotion in his mind was that of guilt, that in some way he had been responsible for what had happened. I wept for the loss of a precious innocence which could never be reclaimed. This sense of guilt and blame had blighted his sexuality for ten years. His story is tragically common; often the abuser is a close family member and sadly the pattern of abuse often repeats itself. The abused becomes the abuser.

As you listen to the story come tumbling out you wonder how far this shame stretches back

As you listen to the story come tumbling out you wonder how far this shame stretches back, and how many generations have been touched by this kind of behaviour. In past times even to mention these secret things was too shocking and too terrible. The emerging statistics of child sexual abuse in the UK are appalling but at least the issue is now being brought into the light where it can be confronted. Nevertheless, the rottenness at the core of our society is very great. In prisons like HMP Hull, the units for special vulnerable prisoners (VPs), kept separately because of the risk of harm from other prisoners, are full to overflowing. Our own VP wing at Doncaster is always full, often with men who have been convicted of crimes committed many years ago.

It can be very depressing working with those convicted of sexual offences. Usually there is a considerable degree of denial. So does God love sex offenders? It is a bald question but a deeply urgent one. I have come to suspect that he does. Why should we ever have doubted? How often we slip into the stance of the older brother standing with pursed lips and tightly clenched hands as the wayward son is welcomed back.

We tend to steer debates away from the discussion of whether or not God wants to forgive those convicted of serious sexual offences, not because we are afraid of debate but because of the overwhelmingly powerful emotions uncovered in the hearts of men who may have been abused themselves or who have been fed a hysterical and sensationalist line by the press. We have VPs who are a valued and accepted part of the chapel fellowship. We passionately proclaim the complete extent of God's forgiveness but we emphasize the need for truth, for the light to shine in the murky places and the need for repentance. We teach that the wrong attitude to sex is a continuum which stretches from soft porn posters, through a typical Sunday night's viewing on BBC TV to Internet hard core and onto acts of great and dark evil. Let us remember that it is a line which is inhabited by all kinds of people. Priests, police officers, doctors, teachers and many other people who would be called pillars of the community have been caught in recent child pornography cases. All across the spectrum there is denial. Our society is saturated with sex and hypocrisy but many social commentators still refuse to accept that we have a deep problem.

Sex offenders do become Christians and they present a challenge

What of the ones who come into God's light? Sex offenders do become Christians and they present a challenge. Not only do they have to seek forgiveness for their sins, but they also have to cope with forgiving what people have done to them and then go on to cope with the hatred of other people towards them. They are usually people with a desperately low self-esteem. But I feel that the promise 'that they will repair the devastations of many generations' is a promise which is for them. Otherwise there is no hope.

Must the abuse go on? Do we simply sigh, shrug our shoulders and plan to manage and minimize the risk? Has the Christian sex offender no hope? Must he automatically fulfil the expectations of once a paedophile always a paedophile, or once a rapist always a rapist? This is the new leprosy. Any church which welcomes one of these into its fold risks the wrath of those who would 'out' these people. Thankfully the Diocese in which I work has a clear policy of disclosure to vicar and wardens and I have seen this policy at work and working. This is good and to the church's credit. HMP Whatton has pioneered a contract for prisoners coming out of the prison to enter into with their sponsoring church. A co-operation between the church, the Probation Officer, and Social Services can, in confidence, deliver safety, social inclusion and dignity.

It is then possible for these Christian lepers to give thanks to God and put an end to generations of devastation. Surely this must be a better and safer way of dealing with these people than the 'outing' called for, where convicted sex offenders are driven out of society into a murky underworld where there is no chance of healing and where there is a considerable danger of re-offending. Alongside the potential stone throwing in glass houses surely must be a realization that sex offenders are nurtured by a society that shamelessly exploits God's precious gift of sex.

Questions for Reflection

1   What is your own attitude to sex offenders?

2   How would you integrate a released sex offender into your church?

3   Sexual abuse is very common. How is your church prepared to help the healing process with victims?

8

An Anointed World

In the middle of Isaiah 61 we come upon a strange, almost imperialistic promise, that 'aliens will tend the flocks of the people of God.'

Am I alone in being troubled by the kind of prophecies that predict prosperity for Israel at the expense of other nations? Perhaps it would be better to skip over passages like this in times of multiculturalism, diversity and interfaith understanding. Yet once again we find ourselves in strange times as unparalleled movements of peoples across the globe take place. At HMP Doncaster we see representatives from many nations: Romanians, Kosovans, Iraqis, Iranians, Portuguese, Jamaicans, Angolans. People arriving after long journeys remind us of the pain and suffering in countries like Iraq, Bosnia and Afghanistan. We have excellent relations with the Muslim community and a healthy respect and dialogue has opened up. We serve each other as professional colleagues and friends who laugh together. Where else do Muslims and Christians do this? It was John V Taylor, thirty years ago, writing in his famous book, *The Go-between God*, who pointed out that the Holy Spirit was quite capable of moving in the hearts of people of different faiths. Maybe in this age where the traditional churches seem to becoming more entrenched and more isolated there is a need for us to understand afresh the capacity of the Spirit to move anywhere, in anybody and at any time.

A brief survey of the Bible will quickly tell us of the Spirit moving in Melchizedek, Cyrus, the wise men from the East and even Balaam's ass! All were from different cultures and faiths but each acted as agents of the living God.

> A is a Farsi speaker and comes from an Islamic background. He is a cultured man with a gentle and enquiring manner. He never expected to serve a prison sentence separated from his family. I cannot quite remember when he appeared in chapel but he has become a regular attender at groups and at worship. His eyesight is not too good and he desperately wanted the Scriptures in Persian. An entry on an Internet search engine immediately threw up an Internet site of Iranian Christians in America and I was able to download portions of Matthew's gospel in Farsi along with a topical magazine. A has begun to attend the *Alpha* course. Last Sunday he came up to me with a glow on his face which had replaced the tears of frustration he previously had had. We had been talking about the Stations of the Cross in the chapel and I had explained to him the last steps that Jesus had taken to his death. During the service we had watched part of the *Jesus* video where the Lord is crucified. A explained to me that his wife had made an extra visit to see him in prison. He told her that he had decided to go to church and instead of scolding him she told him that she had noticed a change in him. We have sent his wife a Farsi Bible too.

Could it be that those whom the world calls aliens or asylum seekers will be the ones who tend the flocks? A local church in Doncaster has been deeply enriched by the growing number of Iranian Christians meeting there. The press and many of the general public see the flow of foreigners as a threat to our culture and way of life but many of them are people of faith and open to the gospel of Christ.

Questions for Reflection

1 Asylum seekers may well enter your church. How would you view them?
2 What practical steps would you be ready to take to help them?
3 Do you accept that the arrival of so many people from so many races and creeds is an opportunity rather than a threat?

9 Anointed as Priests of the Lord

I believe that Isaiah 61 gives clear support to the teaching in 1 Peter 2.8 where Peter speaks of 'the priesthood of all believers.'

It does not support a hierarchical model of priesthood adopted by the Western church since Christianity became the official religion of the Roman Empire.

As *each person* is anointed, the gospel is proclaimed in word and action and we see the train of events predicted by Isaiah. Instead of broken, timid ones, 'You shall be called the priests of the Lord, men shall speak of you as the ministers of the Lord.' I hasten to add that I am not equating this prophecy with a flood of neatly ordained clergyman flooding into the main denominations! The promise is that men and women will move from brokenness, from exile from God, from shame, into a position where they are able to serve the people of God and where 'the priesthood of all believers' is a visible reality.

M is a young man who, at the time of writing, is finishing his three year sentence at an open prison, having spent eighteen months at Doncaster. M is very bright but had fallen into the dominant drug culture like many of his generation in the old coal mining communities in South Yorkshire. Despite a loving home and educational opportunities he turned to crime and served a sentence as a young offender. He had good intentions on release but quickly resumed old acquaintances and soon found himself with another long prison sentence. We met him shortly after his arrival at Doncaster. Quickly he became established as a strong member of St Barnabas Chapel at a time when we were developing the Isaiah vision. He made a commitment to Christ during Easter 2002. I soon noticed that this young man, still only twenty-one years old, had a great flair for communicating a message with depth and simplicity. Traditionally there has been an uncomfortable divide between chaplains and prisoners. Obviously security considerations have always to be held in mind but if we are the body of Christ then we should expect the gifts of the Spirit to be distributed amongst the members of the body.

A gardener can look at a fruit tree in the late Summer and predict how much fruit the tree can potentially grow next year because next year's fruit buds will already have formed on the tree. The task of the leadership is to nurture the buds so that they are fed, watered and allowed to blossom. Therein lies the problem with so much of church life. A young plant needs light, air and support—in shade it will eventually wither. I challenged M to exercise his preaching gift one morning at our early morning prayer service in chapel. He spoke in a way that would not have disgraced many preachers of more advanced experience and years. He has continued to do this.

One talk during Holy Week brought a new dimension about the Cross to us all. M recognizes himself as a criminal who has hurt people. He told us that on the cross Jesus was aware of each sin as it was placed on him, robbery, burglary, murder, sex offences, greed, and hate. It was a shocking thing to say but only someone who has sunk into the depths of crime and drug addiction could speak in this way. Paul taught that 'He who knew no sin was made sin' (2 Cor 5.21). If we say to an individual that Jesus died for your sin, should not we mean the particular sin which that person has committed? We teach, for instance, that pornographic pictures are sinful and that they will ultimately produce a bitter harvest. We teach the need for repentance—take the pictures off the wall—and then the glorious acceptance of forgiveness, new life and freedom from the power of sin. The cross is strong and particular medicine for a serious illness.

A person who has sunk low in crime will be given a fuller appreciation of what it means to be forgiven at the foot of the cross. 'We deserve the punishment we received...Jesus remember me today when you come into your kingdom.' M brought a fresh understanding to us on that Good Friday; it was a holy moment. 'You shall be called priests of the Lord.' We spot the embryonic fruit buds. There must be no delay in placing into the hands of a young man like M the necessary opportunities for those buds to begin to grow, along with the necessary climate and conditions. The story of singer and song-writer, Matt Redman, is precisely an example of this. Trusted as a thirteen year old by his youth leader to write songs and lead worship he progressed from stumbling hesitancy to the position he occupies in world Christian music today. After all, the adults could not face Goliath but David could!

During his time with us M was blessed by mentoring visits from a young clergyman, another role model for M to take on board. We also provided a framework of regular debriefing sessions on difficulties encountered along the way. It was quite surprising how often a young man like M needed to talk about aspects of his growing Christian life such as controlling anger, sexuality and developing an appropriate spirituality. Perhaps the Christian community does not offer enough opportunities to talk and explore for the one who is showing a budding vocation. As a young Christian I was deeply helped by a ready access to wiser and older brothers and sisters in Christ. It was often on the level of 'Can I pop round for a cup of a coffee and a chat.' Lessons shared and learnt nearly thirty years ago still sustain and shape my ministry now.

Research conducted by Martin Robinson of the Bible Society has shown that the weakening of an obvious Christian influence in society has resulted in young people being unable to find those who will answer their spiritual questions. The result is that at least two generations have now internalized spirituality to a private and virtually inaccessible place. Robinson reports on a study conducted in a Birmingham car factory found that three-quarters of the men prayed but not one of them would admit it to their colleagues.[4] Our experience with M and other young men has highlighted the need for open access to those who can answer the questions in a young heart.

M continued over months to develop his skills of communicating the gospel. He has now moved on to an open prison and recently wrote a letter in which he said that he was finding the move away from the close fellowship at HMP Doncaster difficult and that the situation was 'lonely' but that his spiritual resources were deep enough to see him through this challenging situation. On some evenings his room at the prison has resounded with the sound of Christian choruses as ten men crowd in there. 'They have never met anyone like me,' M wrote in his letter. On release M plans to go to a Christian rehabilitation house in London; eventually he hopes to go on to theological study.

Questions for Reflection

1   How would you help someone like M if he came to your church?

2   Are there any ways of making Christian resources available to young people seeking answers to their questions?

3   Think of ways in which your fellowship could better reflect the concept of 'the priesthood of all believers.'

Anointed with Honour **10**

In our journey through Isaiah 61 we have seen that God does not change as he deals with his people.

We can expect the Lord to touch his people with healing, calling his people into wholeness. As this happens dignity is restored. This encapsulates Christian prison ministry. However, much of what happens in prison is a very negative experience. Many convicted prisoners will talk of the shame of standing in the dock in court and the shame of the judge's words as sentence is being passed and the utterance of the ominous words, 'Take him down.'

Fred was 43 years of age when I met him in the Prison Health Centre. Though not a Christian, he had asked to see me. 'I never believed I would ever experience anything like that' he said. 'It was awful. The reception officer said to me, "Who are you?" "Mr Taylor," I replied automatically. "No, you're not," came the immediate reply, "You're Taylor FA26704," It was at that moment that I really felt the full force of being inside.'

Fred described the way in which his few possessions had been searched, his wallet emptied, the photographs of his wife and children carelessly handled. That simple action caused him deep pain. As we talked he reflected on the time in police cells, in the van bringing him to prison, known as 'the sweat box.' When he entered the first of the prison gates the engine had been turned off whilst its security and appropriate paperwork about its 'contents' were given to the gate officer. Before it restarted and before it entered the inner gates Fred said that his heart had raced as he viewed razor wire and high fences from the tiny window of the van. He asked himself, 'When will I next go out?'

He had never been in prison before and now he was being 'processed,' subjected to a 'strip-search' which he saw as the final humiliation as he was 'dehumanized,' stripped of his dignity. 'I felt as if I was being mocked,' he said, 'though no one said a word wrong. The whole procedure just seemed designed to humiliate me. I know it's the system but it's awful.'[5]

In the current climate of retribution and calls for longer sentences, the notion of dignity is not one which many politicians would entertain. The prison experience with its giving of the prison number and the change from human being to inmate is a dehumanizing one. Many think that this is a just punishment for crime. But it is the courts who punish and the prisons are given the task of caring for those who are put there by the courts. A brutal regime has been shown to act less as a deterrent and more as a preparation for further and often more serious crime. An establishment which creates shame amongst its prisoners therefore becomes a seedbed for hate, anger, and despair. The image of HMP Slade and *Porridge* in the 1970s TV programme still lurks in the psyche of the public and some members of the prison service. Prisons that practice an enlightened philosophy of respect whilst also attempting to address offending behaviour, stand a better chance of rehabilitating the offender and making the person aware of the harm that they have caused to their victim.

The change from human being to inmate is a dehumanizing one

Naming and shaming may be a popular catch phrase but it is no answer to the deep-rooted problems of criminal activity we face. It is the facing up to an offence which prepares an offender to change. This seems to be a paradox but it is a core Christian belief that the Holy Spirit will lead the believer into all truth and then that truth will set you free. A person whose faith in Christ gives him dignity is more able to accept that he has sinned and fallen short of God's standards.

The notion of dignity lies at the heart of restorative justice. Ancient societies practised the idea of the perpetrator making amends to the victim for the wrong committed. Today the state intervenes in the process and the offender pays his debt to society. This strips dignity away from the victim and heaps shame on the criminal. The whole process fails to heal the victim and fails to make the offender see the need for some kind of act of restitution. E, whose story is told below, told me that one of the worst aspects of his sentence was the knowledge that he had created another victim. In his case it has not been possible for him to make amends. In other cases involving the mediation service REMEDI, prisoners have been able to meet their victims face to face in a carefully controlled situation. We encourage the Christians in St Barnabas Chapel to think very seriously about making some gesture to their victims. As they do that they often discover that God takes their shame away. Yes, we believe that the moment forgiveness is asked for it is granted by God, but a need to work out that forgiveness in practical action is the path to dignity and a future free from crime.

We often hear men saying that they were glad that God brought them into prison. Some say that they were relieved to be caught so finally they could get out of the nightmare their actions had created. Some of them would strongly agree that the Lord has indeed replaced the shame of drug addiction, thieving and begging with the honour of being part of God's family.

One man, E was charged with a very serious crime. A past offence for which he had served many years was not supposed to be revealed in court but so high was the profile of the case that details slipped into the press. Previous colleagues and friends told the story of how they had known him. The judge, in his summing up, called E an evil and manipulative man who had deceived his friends into supporting him. After sentencing, E arrived in the prison with a long sentence and the words of the judge metaphorically hung round his neck—in reality a double punishment.

E came from a Christian family and shared some of that faith even though, in his own admission he had strayed away in the years he had been out of prison. HMP Doncaster is a short-stay remand prison and unusually E has served nearly two years of his sentence at the prison, but he is looking forward to moving soon as his sentence plan progresses. After the early months of coming to terms with his situation E began to rediscover his faith and deepen it. This process of restoring dignity came in a joyful service where E's family, friends and members of his church witnessed his baptism by full immersion in the chapel of St Barnabas. E is growing in his faith and is an inspiration to others. He is able to use his experience of the dehumanizing process of prison to help those who are fearful first-timers in the system. The way in which he conducted himself with dignity through difficult episodes of the past two years have raised him above the hatred and slurs he received on sentencing. He is able to minister in the name of Jesus to newcomers and those in need of a listening ear.

'I will take their shame away and give them a double portion.' Prison life often dehumanizes but the active Christian love and witness that flows from a chapel community in prison helps broken people to rediscover that they are human beings made in the image of God.

Questions for Reflection

1   Make a list of qualities that give dignity to a human being.

2   How could you help a prisoner or ex-prisoner find these?

3   Are there any ways in which you could put restorative justice into action?

11

Prison ministry is a fast-moving task.

The ministry of Jesus was condensed into just three years and as I approach the three year mark in my ministry at Doncaster I marvel at the number of people I have come across in the path of the chaplaincy. Even during the months that this booklet has taken to come to production, new faces have appeared, familiar ones have moved on, and there have been tragedies and joys. One of our chapel contacts left prison and chose not to go to a rehabilitation house. Three hours later he had died of a drug overdose. Another strong chaplaincy member left prison, seemed to be doing very well, but then stole some money. His story of his past life which had seemed so plausible turned out to be lies.

It is during the disappointments and frustrations that we are moved to turn back to scriptures. Isaiah chapter 61 is an inspiration because at its core are not the actions of sinful people but the gracious movement of an almighty God. The anointing of the Spirit comes in spite of us. Verse 10 says, 'He has clothed me with the garments of salvation.' The inevitable action of God is to cause 'righteousness and praise to spring forth before all the nations.'

Last week M and R accompanied me down to a small Pentecostal tin tabernacle in a nearby coal mining village. The weather was wet and discouraging, the congregation small and solemn. R played some music, M accompanied him on the guitar. I spoke on the theme of hope and the two ex-prisoners spoke briefly about what their former lives had been like. A 12-year-old boy sitting at the front of the meeting butted in with the remark that he was teased at school because he read the Bible and trusted in Jesus. R and M replied that walking onto a wing surrounded by the abuse of other prisoners had made them strong and proud to be Christians. Often the ones who had given that very abuse were the ones who came knocking at the cell door asking for prayer. It was just two years ago that M and R had entered prison as drug addicts, written off by society. We finished the evening feeling that once again God has anointed us with praise and that out of barren soil God had caused righteousness to spring.

A Conclusion

12

'For as the earth brings forth its shoots, and as a garden causes what is sown in it to spring up, so the Lord God will cause righteousness and praise to spring forth before all the nations.'

Our experiences at HMP Doncaster are reproduced many times over at other prisons and probably more so. We have not discovered the holy grail! We are not Christian alchemists whose touch turns everything to a conversion. I have recorded a few examples simply to show that God will always be true to his word and character.

We are simply the gardeners, and God gives the increase

If there is any lesson to learn from our experiences over the past months it is that we can *expect* God to move in response to the prayers of his people. It is in his very nature to cause righteousness and praise to spring up. If I neglect my garden then weeds grow up and the soil becomes untended and ultimately infertile. We are simply the gardeners in our work in St Barnabas, and God gives the increase. Maybe churches should do less and expect more.

Many churches should do less and expect more

At our latest *Alpha* course we began with nine members. At the next session this grew to fourteen even though two from the previous session were not there. The third session had grown to seventeen because the course members were bringing their friends and cell-mates along. As I looked around the group I knew many of the faces because I had previously met them: S could have gone to Betel House[6] a year ago but missed the opportunity and slid back into drugs—he had decided to pop along. D has been around Christian circles for several years but is now ready to move on with God. P came on a bereavement course and has now found Jesus, healing and hope for the future. J went through great turmoil but is now growing in faith and brought four people with him including P, who is a first timer in prison and has not been in church since he was a young man. I met M a year ago when we were talking about Christian rehab.

Prison ministry inside and outside the walls has significantly impacted local churches

Prison ministry inside and outside the walls has significantly impacted local churches. One co-operative venture has been the setting up of a trust, The Restoring Broken Walls Trust, to channel support to prisoners, ex-prisoners and their families. Over one hundred prayer letters go out each month from the prison to supporters. There is a weekly email prayer-note that also goes out to supporters. This is garden maintenance. As we step daily into the garden of St Barnabas HMP Doncaster, we know that the prayer gardeners have already been doing their work because the Lord God causes righteousness and praise to spring up before all the nations.

Questions for Reflection

1 Reflect on the 'garden' where you work. Describe it in terms of soil, weeds, fertility.

2 Consider how you tend it.

3 Think of the expectations (or lack of) you have for your work.

Grant us a vision, Lord
To see what we can achieve
To reach out beyond ourselves
To share our lives with others
To stretch our capabilities
To increase our sense of purpose
To be aware of where we can help
To be sensitive to your Presence
To give heed to your constant call [7]

Appendix: Useful Information

Alpha

An introductory course to the Christian faith. Also: *Prison Alpha* and *Caring for Ex-Offenders.*

Contact: *Alpha* International, Holy Trinity Brompton, Brompton Road, London SW7 1JA. Tel: 0845 644 7544

Web: www.alphacourse.org *and* www.caringforexoffenders.org

William Noblett

William is the current Chaplain General. His book *Prayers for People in Prison* is an inspiring source book on chaplaincy work in prisons. It deals with all aspects of prison life, giving a short and accurate account with a prayer or spiritual reflection at the end of each section. This is a 'must' for all those involved in prison ministry.

Prison Fellowship

An excellent organization that has been working in Britain's prisons for nearly thirty years. Its supporters cover most of the nation's prisons, trains volunteers and provides numerous courses.

Contact: PO Box 945, Maldon, Essex, CM9 4EW.

Beacon House/Rock House Trust

This charity has been up and running for five years and maintains a half way house for ex-offenders and a move on flat.

Contact: 27–29 Beaconsfield Rd, Hexthorpe, Doncaster, South Yorkshire.

Restoring Broken Walls Trust

Support for prisoners, ex-prisoners and their families, including weekly email prayer-note.

Contact: c/o The Chaplaincy, HMP Doncaster, Doncaster, DN5 8UX.

Betel of Britain

Prison rehabilitation through two houses at Nottingham and Birmingham.

Contact: 01564 822356

Remedi

Mediation Service between victims and offenders.

Contact: 342 Glossop Rd, Sheffield, S10 2HW. Tel: 0114 249 3496

Web: www.remedi.cjb.net

If you have any comments or questions—or require further information please email me at philip@iresonr.freeserve.co.uk

---

Notes

1 Philip Yancey, *Finding God in Unexpected Places* (Hodder and Stoughton) p 187.

2 George Lings is a Church Growth specialist with Church Army. His series of pamphlets, *Encounters on the Edge* deal with some of the themes I have raised in a very practical way. Contact details: tel 0114 272 7451; email: g.lings@sheffieldcentre.org.uk

3 Welsh Revival website www.robibrad.demon.co.uk—downloaded: 06.10.03.

4 Martin Robinson, *Faith of the Unbeliever* (Monarch) p 75.

5 William Noblett, *Prayers for People in Prison* (Oxford University Press) p 3.

6 *Betel of Britain* An international organization which has been working to rehabilitate prisoners for many years. It has two houses at Nottingham and Birmingham.

7 David Adam.